ETERNITY

A SURVIVAL GUIDE

STEPHEN E. LEHNERT, MD

WESTBOW
PRESS®
A DIVISION OF THOMAS NELSON
& ZONDERVAN

WestBow Press books may be ordered through booksellers or by contacting:

WestBow Press
A Division of Thomas Nelson & Zondervan
1663 Liberty Drive
Bloomington, IN 47403
www.westbowpress.com
1 (866) 928-1240

Scripture quotations are taken from The New American Standard Bible®, Copyright © 1960, 1962, 1963, 1968, 1971, 1972, 1973, 1975, 1977, 1995 by The Lockman Foundation. Used by permission.

ISBN: 978-1-9736-9637-7 (sc)
ISBN: 978-1-9736-9639-1 (hc)
ISBN: 978-1-9736-9638-4 (e)

Library of Congress Control Number: 2020912853

Print information available on the last page.

WestBow Press rev. date: 07/27/2020

Contents

Author's Note

I am a medical doctor who diagnoses and takes care of physical illness of patients as my vocation. I interpret x-ray images and scans, and I do interventional procedures with needles and place tubes under imaging guidance to provide vein and arterial access, drainage of infected or obstructed organs, provide critical nutrition as well as medications to support life and treat diseases such as infections and cancer. That being said, it has become apparent to me that people are in need in a much more important part of their lives, particularly in the time we are currently living. It has prompted me to write this book, giving important references along the way so that you can go back, reflect on, and seek to learn more of the topic I'm about to discuss.

Preface

If you see danger coming, you want to tell your friends so that they can prepare and protect themselves. That being said, based on conversations I have had with people fairly close to me, it has become apparent that many people are searching for an answer to a question coming from deep within themselves. This question is about their futures, both in this life and their lives after their physical deaths.

It happened one Friday night after dinner and the nightly news. I received a text from my sister-in-law, and the conversation went as follows.

> A: Hi, it's Allison. I have a quick question. I'm writing a paper for my religion class. Is it the same John who wrote the gospel of John and Revelation? I figured you would know.

> S: Yes, John the apostle. Banished to the island of Patmos when he was older, and God revealed the revelation through His angel to the apostle/disciple John.

A: Cool, thanks. One more question. I think it's surprising that the Jews let Christians use their canon since they didn't like the Christians at all.

S: You mean the Old Testament writings/scrolls? Early Christians came from the Jewish people who witnessed Christ's resurrection and fulfilled a large number of the prophecies in their canon (Old Testament). Isaiah 53 in particular.

A: Yeah, the Old Testament. Okay, I'll have that be one of the points in the paper. Thank you for the reference. If you think of any more … It's strange the Jews didn't become Christians then.

S: Isaiah prophesies in Isaiah 6:10 that while seeing physically, they could not see spiritually. And while hearing physically, they could not hear spiritually. In John 3:5-7, Christ told Nicodemus he had to be born again spiritually to understand what He was telling him.

A: That's good stuff, Steve! Thank you.

S: That's the problem with people today. They go all the way through life not realizing they have never been born again into the spiritual life that the Old and New Testaments point to through all the prophets in the Old Testament, and Christ on earth performing miracles, signs, and ultimately being rejected by the Jews and crucified to pay for sins as found in the New Testament. These Jews, who could not see spiritually and finally crucified the actual Son of God. When people accept what Christ did, ask for forgiveness of their sins, and confess Him to others, He brings them to life spiritually. What then happens is that the Holy Spirit comes to dwell in the person and opens up his or her physical mind to understand the spiritual realm that has to do with eternity after we die in our physical bodies. That's why Christians have eternal life and access to the spiritual realm and a supernatural understanding of who God really is. Their funerals are a time of rejoicing rather than grieving. Their consciouses now tells them what's right and wrong. They can live their physical lives in victory knowing they have God Himself with them. I could tell you a whole lot more, but I'm still in the learning phase. I also have to tell you that because of good and evil in the world, true Christians who are born again—and not just labeled as Christians—go through life sometimes experiencing some really tough times because they are dealing with things in the supernatural spiritual realm that those not born again don't understand. But they have God at their sides to protect them and instruct them on what's happening and how to respond. Does that make sense to you?

A: I just got home. I'm going to read your text when I get settled. Thank you. It looks like you wrote the paper for me. LOL.

S: Lately a lot of people have been asking me some serious life questions.

A: I finally got to read your text. Very beautifully put! It's so interesting. I can see that spiritual people probably do have the spiritual realm to battle with too! Remember ***, one of the guys I dated? Well he was very spiritual and knew the Bible front and back. He was interesting to talk to. I remember him saying when you guys adopted the girls that we are going to be a curse to you guys. Isn't that weird?

S: The difference is that people who are not born again spiritually, when faced with battles and great conflicts, don't have the same equipment to battle and get through them, and they often give up in despair or are defeated in their physical lives, not knowing the power available to spiritually reborn people. Spiritually reborn people often know what's happening to them and have a supernatural omnipotent God, who can fight for them not only in the physical realm but also the spiritual, so they are not defeated mentally too.

A: So true!

S: Some spiritual people seek the demonic evil realm—the occult—as described by some and get their powers from the evil one and his angelic beings, although these are not as powerful as the Christ-following omnipotent God's spiritual realm's good angelic beings. The satanic demonic spiritual beings can end up destroying the lives of the nonspiritually reborn. Demons shudder at the power of Christ in the spiritual realm. Most people are oblivious to these things going on around them and sometimes question when tragedy strikes them, looking for answers or reasons. Some do end up turning to Christ and are reborn into the spiritual realm of good, where there is great power. Their lives are then changed for the good, and they can conquer old debilitating habits physically and mentally, and have a new positive outlook on life.

A: Oh yes! I love this time of the year with Easter coming up. It's always fun to watch good Jesus movies now.

S: Yes. If people only knew of what was happening in the background. Boy, you've really caused me to think of some things tonight. I'm thinking of writing a book. This is helping. It's about spiritual growth and awareness.

A: You should for sure write a book. It probably wouldn't take you that long.

S: I know. I happen to have a little extra time now. Well I hope your paper goes well. Let me know if you have any more questions. It will cause me to think about them and look up the answers. From the spiritual realm, that is.

A: Yeah. That's terrible for you guys. Hopefully everything turns out okay. Ha, I will. After this paper I'm writing about the gospel of Thomas.

S: It will turn out the way God has planned it to be. I'm hoping to be able to get back to work soon and support the people God has placed in my life.

A: Yes. Stay positive. I always wondered why Christ said, "God, why have you forsaken me," as His last words. What do you think he meant? Because I think I had a realization about it. Okay, so here's what I think, and then I'll stop bothering you. I think that Christ felt separated from God, death, so he was able to feel human feelings also. Anyway, I'll let you go for the night. Nice talking to you, Steve.

S: He was also human at the time, in addition to being God, and He had that intense separation momentarily from His loving Father. He now sits at the right hand of power in the heavenly spiritual realm with God Himself, who dwells in unapproachable light due to the magnitude of His greatness. Do you realize you can communicate with this God in prayer as a born-again Christian? Nice talking to you too. This has helped me with the book I'm trying to write. Have a nice night.

A: Good to hear. Everything you said is very powerful. And your passion about Jesus makes it come alive!

S: Not to scare you but you mentioned *** knowing the Bible in and out. I think Satan probably knows the Bible in and out too. He used Bible verses to tempt Christ in the wilderness, but in the wrong way, through misinterpretation. Satan even sometimes disguised himself as an angel of light in the church, among Christian followers (2 Corinthians 11:14). That's why in 1 John 4:1-6 it says we're supposed to test the spirits to see if they are from God. So it doesn't surprise me what *** said.

A: Yeah, that's scary! LOL. Luckily I have good sense of humor and do not get too concerned about my past.

S: Yes, as a Christian you will ultimately overcome evil through Christ. Psalm 16:11—I'll leave you with that verse to think about. It involves spending eternity with God.

At the end of this text conversation, I started thinking about people in general.

I've noticed that many questions become apparent when we have stresses and troubles in life that are seemingly out of control. I guess the ultimate stress would be when encountering coming close to physical death. I think many questions and thoughts would start to flood your mind to the point of wondering why you have never thought of them before this critical time. What will happen to me? What will happen to my loved ones? Is this all there is to life? I'm scared. Is this all there is to it? What's going to happen? Will I just fall asleep? What if there is something after death that I don't know about? Do I need a preacher or priest here to help me? Have I lived a good enough life? Why is this happening to me? Nobody ever told me about this, what to expect, or how hard it is. I'm really scared. I'm in pain. I'm having trouble breathing. I'm starting not to think straight. What if I missed out on something really important that nobody told me about?

After thinking about some of these things, let's try to answer some questions. My hope is that the questions in the following chapter will serve as a framework for you to come back to often. And then to research each question more as you see fit and with the level of interest you have. I start answering these questions with the basic truths as I know them and ask you to delve further into them and confirm them as needed.

I will go to the best source that has been tried and tested throughout the ages and gives hope and assurance that we are on the right track and not just doing some mental gymnastics. Come with me on this short journey and consider the following.

Chapter 1

ANSWERS TO THE QUESTIONS OF LIFE

Consider the following:

> What is time?
>
> Who are we?
>
> Why are we here?
>
> What is life?
>
> What has happened in the past, now, and in the future?
>
> Who are we in the scope of the universe and creation as we know them?
>
> What governs the laws of the physical and spiritual universe?
>
> What is eternity?
>
> What are critical points of awareness to humans?

What gives the authors of the Bible the authority to talk about these things?

What type of people and their responses show they have knowledge of these revealed things?

What is spiritual rebirth? What age does spiritual rebirth start?

What should our responses be? How should we live after a spiritual rebirth?

What is happening in the spiritual realm? What is the spiritual realm as it relates to the physical?

What are spiritual battles? Who and what are involved?

What happens when something goes wrong?

What are we worth?

How should we live?

Finally, what do we have to look forward to?

I invite you to take a journey with me to find answers to these questions regarding how they will affect us for all time. Please note that the seventy years—or eighty years if we have good health—we are here on earth (Psalm 90:10) is just a speck of time in the scope of eternity. But it is actually a testing ground for what we will be involved in for a much greater period of time.

Are you interested?

Let's get started.

Chapter 2

WE ARE CONSCIOUS; WE ARE HERE

Why are you here?

If you take a moment to really think about it, what does your life consist of? You probably have some sort of routine where you get up every day and have some purpose or goal. The first is getting up, and getting cleaned up and dressed. There are many pathways from there. A large majority of people head off to work to provide some type of service or material things for others, thereby receiving an income to take care of themselves.

Many children are under the protection of their parents or others. They are in the early phases of education, learning skills to support themselves later in life. Others are past their working years and in "retirement," which has multiple and varying shapes and forms. It often depends on how and what they did during the educational and work phases of their lives. Some have families, some are single, some have friends, while some are alone.

Our interactions with our environment, personalities, and what we like to do vary considerably among us. This is what makes up the society we live in. Our time away from these activities are needed to provide support for us mentally, physically, socially, and emotionally. This time can be spent in various ways, including hobbies, travel, and get-togethers with others having similar interests.

Then there is the spiritual part of us. Many times it is not thought about very often. It can be confusing to some. And to others, it is basically unknown.

Have you ever wondered why you are here? Why you came into existence? What is the reason you were created? What is your function as it relates to you and to others? How do you affect others? What is your purpose, your value, your worth?

Pain, pleasure, work, and relationships are incidental, personal, and/or intimate. What do you think about throughout the day when you're not directly focused on the task at hand? Are you fixated on one thing? Are you thinking about multiple topics or tasks? Do you have strong emotions or feelings in social interactions with others? How are you efficient with your time? Are you totally focused on work to the extent that you suffer in relationships with your family and others? Will serious events in your life cause your priorities to change?

I ask you now to consider and focus on the spiritual as we look into eternity and what it holds for us.

I purposely kept this book short so that one could read through it and grasp the major questions and concepts. I encourage you to go back and look up and read the referenced scriptural verses, and then with your mind, personality, and spirit think through these questions to find and confirm your own answers. This process tends to aid in remembering things that will help you and when others ask you these questions in the future.

Chapter 3

THE URGENT DECISION

First the ground rules.

I have been spiritually reborn and have the indwelling Holy Spirit as a guide to convict me of sin, righteousness, and judgment as well as reveal God's will for my life.

And He, when He comes, will convict the world concerning sin and righteousness and judgement (John 16:8)

I have come to know the Bible, which has been around for thousands of years, as the Word of God revealed to prophets who were led by this Holy Spirit. It is the reference for truth.

I use the New American Standard Bible as I feel it translates the original Hebrew writings in the Old Testament and the Greek writings in the New Testament. Scholars having painstakingly translated the original text with its grammatical nuances very accurately.

This Bible has the answers needed to understand the questions people have about their lives and eternity.

All Scripture is inspired by God and profitable for teaching, for reproof, for correction, for training in righteousness; so that the man of God may be adequate, equipped for every good work (2 Timothy 3:16-17).

Be diligent to present yourself approved to God as a workman who does not need to be ashamed, accurately handling the word of truth (2 Timothy 2:15).

Christ's followers have a supernatural ability.

This is the promise which He Himself made to us: eternal life. These things I have written to you concerning those who are trying to deceive you. As for you, the anointing which you received from Him abides in you, and you have no need for anyone to teach you; but as His anointing teaches you about all things, and is true and is not a lie, and just as it has taught you, you abide in Him (1 John 2:25-27).

But a natural man does not accept the things of the Spirit of God, for they are foolishness to him; and he cannot understand them, because they are spiritually appraised. But he who is spiritual appraises all things, yet he himself is appraised by no one. For who has known the mind of the Lord that he will instruct Him? But we have the mind of Christ (1 Corinthians 2:14-16).

Please note that this cannot be understood unless a person is spiritually reborn. This appears as foolishness to the spiritually unborn.

For the word of the cross is foolishness to those who are perishing, but to us who are being saved it is the power of God.

For it is written, "I will destroy the wisdom of the wise. And the cleverness of the clever I will set aside." Where is the wise man? Where is the scribe? Where is the debater of this age? Has not God made foolish the wisdom of the world? For since in the wisdom of God the world through its wisdom did not come to know God. God was well-pleased through the foolishness of the message preached to save those who believe. For indeed the Jews ask for signs and Greeks search for wisdom; but we preach Christ crucified, to Jews a stumbling block and to Gentiles foolishness, but to those who are the called, both Jews and Greeks, Christ the power of God and the wisdom of God. Because the foolishness of God is wiser than men, and the weakness of God is stronger than men (1 Corinthians 1:18-25).

I make use of scriptural references throughout this book. Note them throughout because again, the inerrant Word of God as recorded in the scriptures is the basis for truth.

Why am I writing this book?

Ezekiel 33:1-7 provides an alarming answer.

And the word of the Lord came to me, saying, "Son of man, speak to the sons of your people and say to them, 'If I bring a sword upon a land, and the people of the land take one man from among them and make him their watchman, and he sees the sword coming upon the land and blows on the trumpet and warns the people, then he who hears the sound of the trumpet and does not take warning, and a sword comes and takes him away, his blood will be on his own head. He heard the sound of the trumpet but did not take warning; his blood will be on himself.

But had he taken warning, he would have delivered his life. But if the watchmen sees the sword coming and does not blow the trumpet and the people are not warned, and a sword comes and takes a person from them, he is taken away in his iniquity; but his blood I will require from the watchman's hand.' "Now as for you, son of man, I have appointed you a watchman for the house of Israel; so you will hear a message from My mouth and give them warning from Me (Ezekiel 33:1-7).

If I know something that will help others and don't reveal it to them, I am accountable.

My "trumpet sound" to you is the following.

The following verses provide the key to salvation and eternal life: being born again!

"For God so loved the world, that He gave His only begotten Son, that whoever believes in Him shall not perish, but have eternal life (John 3:16).

For Moses writes that the man who practices the righteousness which is based on the law shall live by that righteousness. But the righteousness based on faith speaks as follows: "Do not say in your heart, 'Who will ascend into heaven?' (that is, to bring Christ down), or 'Who will descend into the abyss?' (that is to bring Christ up from the dead)." But what does it say? "The word is near you, in your mouth and in your heart" – that is, the word of faith which we are preaching, that if you confess with your mouth Jesus as Lord, and believe in your heart that God raised Him from the dead, you will be saved; for with the heart a person believes, resulting in righteousness, and with the mouth he confesses, resulting in salvation. For the Scripture says,

"Whoever believes in Him will not be disappointed." For there is no distinction between Jew and Greek; for the same Lord is Lord of all, abounding in riches for all who call on Him; for whoever will call on the name of the Lord will be saved." How will they call on Him in whom they have not believed? How will they believe in Him whom they have not heard? And how will they hear without a preacher? How will they preach unless they are sent? Just as it is written, "How beautiful are the feet of those who bring good news of good things!" However, they did not all heed the good news; for Isaiah says, "Lord who has believed our report?" So faith comes from hearing, and hearing by the word of Christ (Romans 10: 5-17).

More information can be found in John 6:40; Ephesians 2:8-9; 2 Corinthians 5:17.

For this is the will of My Father, that everyone who beholds the Son and believes in Him will have eternal life, and I Myself will raise him up on the last day (John 6:40)."

For by grace you have been saved through faith; and that not of yourselves, it is the gift of God; not as a result of works, so that no one may boast (Ephesians 2:8-9).

Therefore if anyone is in Christ, he is a new creature, the old things passed away; behold, new things have come (2 Corinthians 5:17).

As you will see, this is a requirement to even understand what I'm talking about. It is the deciding time in a person's physical life, critical point of awareness, that determines the course of his or her eternal life. This is the spiritual rebirth. I cannot stress this point enough. If you are confused, please come back to these verses.

In your mind/conscious, ask God to reveal these things to you. Accept His invitation to life eternal by faithfully believing in Jesus Christ. His Holy Spirit will prompt you to make this decision.

For those of you who remember the evangelist Billy Graham, he would often quote the following.

Multitudes, multitudes in the valley of decision! For the day of the Lord is near in the valley of decision (Joel 3:14).

I feel called to write and tell you about these things. It is my hope that you will be:

- Born again in the spiritual realm
- Live an amazing life here on earth, both physically and spiritually
- Aware of your surroundings
- Develop goals that will serve you well into eternity. For we are His workmanship, created in Christ Jesus for good works, which God prepared beforehand so that we should walk in them (Ephesians 2:10).
- Have rewards in the eternal realm so that you will be given amazing things to do in eternity. Concerning the parable of the talents (Matthew 25:14-30), the judgement (Matthew 25:31-46), and foundations for living;

According to the grace of God that was given to me, like a wise master builder I laid a foundation, and another is building on it. But each man must be careful how he builds on it. For no man can lay a foundation other than the one which is laid, which is Jesus Christ. Now if any man builds on the foundation with gold, silver, precious stones, wood, hay, straw, each man's work will become evident; for the day will show it because it is to be revealed with fire, and the fire itself will test the quality of each man's work. If any man's work which he has built on it remains, he will receive a reward. If any man's work is burned up, he will suffer loss; but he himself will be saved, yet so as through fire (1 Corinthians 3:10-15).

Although what I just said may seem a bit strange at first, I hope by the end of this book you can see the reality of it. You will have a new supernatural awareness of your surroundings, situations, goals, and dreams in this current physical life. And you will be preparing yourself for a much longer and potentially amazing life in the future. I don't want you to come to the end of your physical life with regrets.

Where are the answers found?

According to the Bible, a man named Paul, who was given special visions and revelations and indwelt by the Holy Spirit, says that the true knowledge of God's mystery is hidden in Jesus Christ Himself, as is hidden all the treasures of wisdom and knowledge (Colossians 2:2-3).

Paul was initially persecuting Jesus and Jesus appeared to him and said 'I am Jesus whom you are persecuting. But get up and stand on your feet; for this purpose I have appeared to you, to appoint you a minister and a witness not only to the things which you have seen, but also to the things in which I will appear to you; rescuing you from the Jewish people and from the Gentiles, to whom I am sending you, to open their eyes so that they may turn from darkness to light and from the dominion of Satan to God, that they may receive forgiveness of sins and an inheritance among those who have been sanctified by faith in Me' (Acts 26:12-18).

Paul was set apart for this purpose to bring the good news to others.

But when God, who had set me apart even from my mother's womb and called me through His grace, was pleased to reveal His Son in me so that I might preach Him among the Gentiles, I did not immediately consult with flesh and blood, nor did I go up to Jerusalem to those who were apostles before me; but I went away to Arabia, and returned once more to Damascus. Then three years later I went up to Jerusalem to become acquainted with Cephas, and stayed with him fifteen days. But I did not see any other of the apostles except James, the Lord's brother. (Now in what I am writing to you, I assure you before God that I am not lying.) Then I went into the regions of Syria and Cilicia. I was still unknown by sight to the churches of Judea which were in Christ; but only they kept hearing, "He who once persecuted us is now preaching the faith which he once tried to destroy." And they were glorifying God because of me (Galatians 1:15-24).

Solomon, the wisest man on earth at the time, listed the usefulness of Proverbs and knowledge in the following.

The proverbs of Solomon the son of David, king of Israel: To know wisdom and instruction, to discern the sayings of understanding, to receive instruction in wise behavior, righteousness, justice and equity; to give prudence to the naive, to the youth knowledge and discretion, a wise man will hear and increase in learning, and a man of understanding will acquire wise counsel, to understand a proverb and a figure, the words of the wise and their riddles. The fear of the Lord is the beginning of knowledge; fools despise wisdom and instruction (Proverbs 1:1-7).

For the Lord gives wisdom; from His mouth come knowledge and understanding (Proverbs 2:6).

Trust in the Lord with all your heart and do not lean on your own understanding. In all your ways acknowledge Him, and He will make your paths straight. Do not be wise in your own eyes; fear the Lord and turn away from evil. It will be healing to your body and refreshment to your bones (Proverbs 3:5-8).

He came to the ultimate conclusion after assessing the vanity of life throughout the book of Ecclesiastes. He talks about life with its works, desires, and longings. His philosophical insight comes to the conclusion, "vanity of vanities" with this life. And then finally in Ecclesiastes 12:13-14 The conclusion, when all has been heard, is: fear God and keep His commandments, because this applies to every person. For God will bring every act to judgement, everything which is hidden, whether it is good or evil.

Jesus Christ came to earth as an exact representation of who God is.

And He is the radiance of His glory and the exact representation of His nature, and upholds all things by the word of His power. When He had made purification of sins, He sat down at the right hand of the Majesty on high (Hebrews 1:3)

Philip said to Him, "Lord, show us the Father, and it is enough for us." Jesus said to him, "Have I been so long with you, and yet you have not come to know Me, Philip? He who has seen Me has seen the Father; how can you say, 'Show us the Father'? (John 14:8-9)

The apostle Paul then described what we can do that is not in vain in this life.

Therefore, my beloved brethren, be steadfast, immovable, always abounding in the work of the Lord, knowing that your toil is not in vain in the Lord (1 Corinthians 15:58).

Realizing and not doing vain things is one of the clear goals of a person who has been born again.

Chapter 4

QUESTIONS ABOUT OUR EXISTENCE

Who is God?

> In the beginning God created the heavens and the earth (Genesis 1:1).

> He who is the blessed and only Sovereign, the King of kings, and Lord of lords, who alone possesses immortality and dwells in unapproachable light, whom no man has seen or can see. To Him be honor and eternal dominion (1 Timothy 6:15, 16).

Who are you?

Then God said, "Let Us make man in Our image, according to Our likeness; and let them rule over the fish of the sea and over the birds of the sky and over the cattle and over all the earth, and over every creeping thing that creeps on the earth. God created man in His own image. In the image of God He created him; male and female He created them (Genesis 1:26, 27).

What is life?

There are two births. One is physical from our parents, and the other is spiritual. A ruler of the Jews asked this question to Jesus when He was on earth approximately two thousand years ago. Jesus told him that unless one is born again, he cannot see the kingdom of God (John 3:3). Jesus also said unless one is born of water (physical) and the Spirit (spiritual), he cannot enter into the kingdom of God (John 3:5).

We have spirits, souls, and bodies.

Now may the God of peace Himself sanctify you entirely; and may your spirit and soul and body be preserved complete, without blame at the coming of our Lord Jesus Christ (1 Thessalonians 5:23).

Therefore if anyone is in Christ, he is a new creature; the old things passed away; behold, new things have come. (2 Corinthians 5:17).

Why are there good and evil forces in the physical and spiritual realms?

In the spiritual realm, evil began from angelic rebellion against the Creator. Man was tempted, sinned, and became aware of his sin in the garden. It now affects us physically and spiritually in a major way. God required in His perfection to send His Son here to earth to live as a perfect human and bear the penalty of our sins for us so that we can be reunited with God in the eternal realm. Temple animal and grain sacrifices in the Old Testament by the Jewish people are earthly examples of what Jesus Christ has done in the spiritual realm in the New Testament for us as a sacrifice—or payment—for our sins.

What is death?

Physical death is the result of sin that entered into the human race shortly after man was created due to temptation and deception from the evil one. It is the cessation of physical body functions on Planet Earth and the cessation or loss of a person's ability to be born into the spiritual realm.

What is time?

Why are dates labeled BC and AD? Who is time based on and referenced to?

B.C. – before Christ; A.D. anno domini – in the year of our Lord.

Otherwise, He would have needed to suffer often since the foundation of the world; but now once at the consummation of the ages He has been manifested to put away sin by the sacrifice of Himself (Hebrews 9:26)

There is an appointed time for everything. And there is a time for every event under heaven—

A time to give birth and a time to die; A time to plant and a time to uproot what is planted.

A time to kill and a time to heal; A time to tear down and a time to build up.

A time to weep and a time to laugh; A time to mourn and a time to dance.

A time to throw stones and a time to gather stones; A time to embrace and a time to shun embracing.

A time to search and a time to give up as lost; A time to keep and a time to throw away.

A time to tear apart and a time to sew together; A time to be silent and a time to speak.

A time to love and a time to hate; A time for war and a time for peace.

What profit is there to the worker from that in which he toils? I have seen the task which God has given the sons of men with which to occupy themselves. He has made everything appropriate in its time. He has also set eternity in their heart, yet so that man will not find out the work which God has done from the beginning even to the end.

I know that there is nothing better for them than to rejoice and to do good in one's lifetime; moreover, that every man who eats and drinks sees good in all his labor—it is the gift of God. I know that everything God does will remain forever; there is nothing to add to it and there is nothing to take from it, for God has so worked that men should fear Him. That which is has been already and that which will be has already been, for God seeks what has passed by (Ecclesiastes 3:1-15).

Time is a measurement. It can seem to go fast or slow. It is a matter of perspective. It is relative according to Albert Einstein. It cannot be recovered in human terms. Once it has passed, the future instantaneously appears, making it the present. Choices, decisions, and actions, laws of the physical universe, creativity, thought, and purposeful and nonpurposeful actions effect outcomes, which can be good or bad.

Where do we get the definitions for right and wrong? What sets the standard or anchor of right and wrong, and by who's definition? How do we understand these things or the difference in right and wrong? For the spiritually born again, the Holy Spirit reveals these things to us in our consciences. (John 16:8)

Let's look at a physical timeline.

Physical timeline

	80	Health issues
		End of life preparation
Elder		Downsizing
	70	
		Grandchildren
		Retirement and/or cutting back on work
Mature adult		
		Children growing up and leaving home
	50	
		Advancing in vocation
Middle age		
		Raising a family, children
		Relationships
	30	
		Vocation-job
Young adult		
		Training-education
	18	
Childhood		School
Physical birth	0	Body, soul, spirit
Conception		

Chapter 5

THE PHYSICAL UNIVERSE CONTRASTED WITH THE SPIRITUAL UNIVERSE

Who are we in the scope of the universe and creation as we know it?

In the beginning God created the heavens and the earth (Genesis 1:1).

If you think about the smallest to largest things you know of, what comes to mind? Tiny subatomic particles (CERN accelerator splitting atoms apart) with 3.5 tetra-electron volts of energy accelerating protons to collide with other protons, producing subatomic particles like quarks and gluons, and recently the Higgs boson to galaxies 2.9 billion light years away (Hubble telescope)? Things around you, tiny insects to giant skyscrapers? How about invisible things like radio waves (AM/FM radio), infrared, ultraviolet, microwave, x-rays, cosmic radiation, and gravitational waves? Things our normal senses do not see apart from special equipment that translates these things into auditory or visual information that we can perceive.

The heavens are telling of the glory of God; And their expanse is declaring the work of His hands. Day to day pours forth speech, And night to night reveals knowledge. There is no speech, nor are there words; Their voice is not heard. Their line has gone through all the earth, and their utterances to the end of the world. In them He has place a tent for the sun, (Psalm 19:1-4)

To Him who made the great lights, for His lovingkindness is everlasting: The sun to rule by day, for His lovingkindness is everlasting, the moon and the stars to rule by night, for His lovingkindness is everlasting (Psalm 136:7-9).

Think for a moment what it would be like if the people inspired by God to write the Old and New Testaments described things that we see today as if they knew then that some of these things exist and work as we see them today. The earth rotating around the sun.

Their line has gone out through all the earth, and their utterances to the end of the world, in them He has placed a tent for the sun, which is as a bridegroom coming out of his chamber; it rejoices as a strong man to run his course. Its rising from one end of the heavens, and its circuit to the other end of them; and there is nothing hidden from its heat (Psalm 19:4-6).

Consider radio waves, ultraviolet, microwaves, gamma x-ray and cosmic rays. (Psalm 19:2-3) The fact that energy is related to mass and the immense power hidden in small things, atomic and hydrogen bombs splitting and fusing atoms in small quantities of material and creating immense amounts of energy.

He who is the blessed and only Sovereign, the King of kings and Lord of lords, who alone possesses immortality and dwells in unapproachable light, whom no man has seen or can see. To Him be honor and eternal dominion! Amen (1 Timothy 6:15-16).

What about things that are yet to be discovered? What about the mind of man that gives him the creativity to investigate these things and put thoughts together to understand them? Can you imagine apostles and disciples in the New Testament seeing a Caterpillar tractor, cranes, bridge-building equipment, and skyscrapers? Can you imagine seeing a F-22 raptor jet or a F-35 lightning II jet thundering through the skies and deploying weapons of destruction as a disciple banished to an island and writing the book of Revelation tries to describe things happening in the end times before the return of Christ? Can you imagine the internet and connectivity of people and their thoughts throughout the world almost instantaneously?

"But as for you, Daniel, conceal these words and seal up the book until the end of time; many will go back and forth, and knowledge will increase (Daniel 12:4)."

This gospel of the kingdom shall be preached in the whole world as a testimony to the nations, and then the end will come (Matthew 24:14).

As a medical doctor, I was required to take a course in college on embryology, which follows the development of a human being from the combining of a sperm and egg into one cell. The cell then multiplies and develops in a specific sequence throughout the pregnancy into a human being as we know it as it travels through the fallopian tube into the uterus of a woman. How the DNA and resultant RNA templates are meticulously programmed to divide and form in a specific set of patterns by proteins with infoldings and cellular movements to create all the complex organs and body forms to create a living and viable human being. Brain, neck, chest, abdomen, pelvis, and extremities all form and can be seen in real time using ultrasound scanning in their early form at six weeks in the mother's body. Can you imagine what David, the psalmist who wrote many of the psalms as inspired by God, would think if he could see these things as we do?

For You have formed my inward parts; You wove me in my mother's womb. I will give thanks to You, for I am fearfully and wonderfully made; wonderful are Your works, and my soul knows it very well. My frame was not hidden from You, when I was made in secret, and skillfully wrought in the depths of the earth; Your eyes have seen my unformed substance; and in Your book were all written the days that were ordained for me, when as yet there was not one of them (Psalm 139:13-16).

The complex equations of mathematics, chemistry, and physics design materials to build things, including computers to do myriad calculations and build complex scanning machines such as CT and MRI scanners to electronically slice a human body like a loaf of bread, producing images to interpret disease states. The patient walks away from the scanner after having one's most inner parts seen with images available to detect internal abnormalities developing before the eye or ear can see them with a stethoscope or physical exam. Constant and almost instantaneous social interactions occur electronically over the World Wide Web through platforms like Facebook, Twitter, Instagram, and Snapchat. Video and audio abilities allow the exchange ideas and plans, as well as to hold meetings.

I could go on and on, but do you see what is being revealed to us in this twenty-first century? Do not lose sight of the fact that our Creator is coming again to evaluate first if we have faith and are born again, and then to examine our works here on earth.

What governs (laws of) the physical and spiritual universe?

We have the study of physics and mathematics to tell and show us the laws of the physical universe. Start with Sir Isaac Newton and his apple falling from the tree (gravity) and progress to theories of relatively relating energy, mass, speed, and gravitational forces.

Let's now turn to the spiritual universe. Using the Bible as a reference, there are many things going on in the background that we don't see. Some people try to discern these things with their physical senses and gadgets they build supposedly to detect movements or signs that these supernatural things, beings, or creatures exist—the study of the paranormal. Many scary movies are made to entertain people in this regard.

The truth of the matter is there is an angelic realm with good angels and bad angels (demons). They serve either God the Creator or Satan, a fallen angel who rebelled against God. These supernatural beings, which are rarely seen by our senses (vision and hearing), rarely appeared to people as recorded in the Bible. There are supernatural battles going on around us that we often don't have a clue about until tragedy strikes or some unusual event affects us or those around us. These events are very difficult to explain from our natural thinking of cause and effect. On deeper investigation in the spiritual realm, these things sometimes become apparent to those with spiritual discernment. But many times they may still be hidden to those even with spiritual discernment. God reveals these spiritual things to born-again believers in Christ as He sees need. The unborn again don't have even a clue of what may be happening. Christ followers—born-again—people face battles that wage war against their minds and thoughts about their beliefs, faiths, and the hopes they have for the future.

For our struggle is not against flesh and blood, but against the rulers, against the powers, against the world forces of this darkness, against the spiritual forces of wickedness in the heavenly places (Ephesians 6:12).

'To open their eyes so that they may turn form darkness to light and from the dominion of Satan to God, that they may receive forgiveness of sins and an inheritance among those who have been sanctified by faith in Me (Acts 26:18).'

There is information on how to take on the armor of God (Ephesians 6:10-17). More on this later.

Chapter 6

PLANTING, GERMINATING, GROWING, AND FRUITING

What type of people have knowledge of these revealed things, and what responses do they show? Read Mark 4:1-20 and Romans 10:8-17.

When Christ was on earth, He often spoke in parables. In some of these parables, He explained the spiritual meaning to His disciples and also for our instruction so that people who had not been spiritually reborn could have a glimpse into the heavenly realm—meaning of these things that normally would be spiritually appraised. An example is the parable of the sower. The sower went out and scattered seeds for a crop, and some of the seeds fell on different kinds of ground and, therefore, grew in different ways because of the available nutrients, water, and type of soil where they fell.

Christ compared this to the way His Word is received in the spirits of people and the effect it has on their lives.

He began to teach again by the sea. And such a very large crowd gathered to Him that He got into a boat in the sea and sat down; and the whole crowd was by the sea on the land. And He was teaching them many things in parables, and was saying to them in His teaching, "Listen to this! Behold, the sower went out to sow; as he was sowing, some seed fell beside the road, and the birds came and ate it up. Other seed fell on the rocky ground where it did not have much soil; and immediately it sprang up because it had no depth of soil. And after the sun had risen, it was scorched; and because it had no root, it withered away. Other seed fell among the thorns, and the thorns came up and choked it, and it yielded no crop. Other seed fell into the good soil, and as they grew up and increased, they yielded a crop and produced thirty, sixty and a hundredfold." And He was saying, "He who has ears to hear, let him hear." As soon as He was alone, His followers, along with the twelve, began asking Him about the parables. And He was saying to them, "To you has been given the mystery of the kingdom of God, but those who are outside get everything in parables, so that while seeing, they may see and not perceive, and while hearing, they may hear and not understand, otherwise they might return and be forgiven." And He said to them, "Do you not understand this parable? How will you understand all the parables? The sower sows the word. These are the ones who are beside the road where the word is sown; and when they hear, immediately Satan comes and takes away the word which has been sown in them. In a similar way these are the ones on whom seed was sown on the rocky places, who, when they hear the word, immediately receive it with joy; and they have no firm root in themselves, but are only temporary; then, when affliction or persecution arises because of the word, immediately they fall away. And others are the ones on whom seed was sown among the thorns; these are the ones who have heard the word, but the worries of the world, and the deceitfulness of riches, and the desires of other things enter in and choke the word, and it becomes unfruitful. And those are the ones on whom seed was sown on the good soil; and they hear the word and accept it and bear fruit, thirty, sixty and a hundredfold (Mark 4:1-20)."

Note the four types of soil or hearts of people He talks about in Mark 4:1-20. See the comparisons He makes to the ground and the different ways people hear the Word and respond. The ultimate goal is to produce crops or good works. Depending on the soil, the plants or the Word may be taken away by the evil one, choked, and not produce fruit or produce fruit in varying degrees. To the extent that we grow spiritually and sink our roots deep into the good soil, we will produce the fruits of the Spirit.

But the fruit of the Spirit is love, joy, peace, patience, kindness, goodness, faithfulness, gentleness, self-control; against such things there is no law (Galatians 5:22-23). And about doing good deeds for others and receive eternal rewards, read Matthew 25:35-40. These are compared to gold, silver and precious stones instead of things that don't last, like wood, hay, and straw, figuratively speaking. (1 Corinthians 3:11-15)

It is all about how we respond when we hear the spiritual life-giving Word of God.

Is everybody born again spiritually? If not, how are you born again spiritually? John 3:16 and 1 John 2:25 explains this. What happens when you're born again spiritually, and what happens if you're not?

How can I write this book and try to explain these things?

First, it is impossible to talk about or have the proper insight into these things unless you have been spiritually reborn (1 Corinthians 1:18-25, 30).

Second, Paul talks about wisdom and faith.

And my message and my preaching were not in persuasive words of wisdom, but in demonstration of the Spirit and of power, so that your faith would not rest on the wisdom of men, but on the power of God (1 Corinthians 2:4-5).

And he talks about the wisdom that will exist in eternity.

Yet we do speak wisdom among those who are mature; a wisdom, however, not of this age nor of the rulers of this age, who are passing away; but we speak God's wisdom in a mystery, the hidden wisdom which God predestined before the ages to our glory; the wisdom which none of the rulers of this age has understood; for if they had understood it they would not have crucified the Lord of glory; but just as it is written, "Things which eye has not seen and ear has not heard, and which have not entered the heart of man, all that God has prepared for those who love Him (1 Corinthians 2:6-9)."

Paul shares how God has revealed this wisdom in spiritual thoughts and spiritual words.

For to us God revealed them through the Spirit; for the Spirit searches all things, even the depths of God. For who among men knows the thoughts of a man except the spirit of the man which is in him? Even so the thoughts of God no one knows except the Spirit of God. Now we have received, not the spirit of the world, but the Spirit who is from God, so that we may know the things freely given to us by God, which things we also speak, not in words taught by human wisdom, but in those taught by the Spirit, combining spiritual thoughts with spiritual words (1 Corinthians 2:10-13).

Please note that a natural person, one who is not reborn in the Spirit, cannot understand these things. They are foolishness to those who have not been reborn in the spiritual world.

And finally, when one is reborn and alive spiritually, he or she can appraise all things. We who are reborn actually have the mind of Christ; the Holy Spirit indwelling in our spirits.

But a natural man does not accept the things of the Spirit of God, for they are foolishness to him; and he cannot understand them, because they are spiritually appraised. But he who is spiritual appraises all things, yet he himself is appraised by no one. For who has known the mind of the Lord, that he will instruct Him? But we have the mind of Christ (1 Corinthians 2:14-16).

What is eternal life?

Eternal life focuses on the spiritual. This is unending, forever. We will also have bodies that people will recognize but in a new form.

There are also heavenly and earthly bodies, but the glory of the heavenly is one, and the glory of the earthly is another. There is one glory of the sun, and another glory of the moon, and another glory of the stars; for star differ from star in glory. So also is the resurrection of the dead. It is sown a perishable body, it is raised and imperishable body; it is sown in dishonor, it is raised in glory; it is sown in weakness, it is raised in power; it is sown a natural body, it is raised a spiritual body. If there is a natural body, there is also a spiritual body. So also it is written, "The first man, Adam, became a living soul." The last Adam became a life-giving spirit. However, the spiritual is not first, but the natural; then the spiritual. The first man is from the earth, earthy; the second man is from heaven. As is the earthy, so also are those who are earthy; and as is the heavenly, so also are those who are heavenly. Just as we have borne the image of the earthy, we will also bear the image of the heavenly (1 Corinthians 15:40-49).

Chapter 7

SPIRITUAL REBIRTH

At what age does spiritual rebirth start?

Please note that this is typically not at the time of your physical birth. It actually may occur at any time throughout your physical life once you have the ability to differentiate right from wrong internally and are prompted by the Spirit of God that you need a spiritual rebirth. Some are born again spiritually at a young age, like six years old. Others receive the call or prompt internally during their grade school or high school years. Some during their early adulthood, and some later in life.

For example, consider the example given in the New Testament of Nicodemus (John 3:3-7). Nicodemus was an older man, a ruler of the Jews, the people Jesus Christ came from. He had heard and seen some of the things Christ was doing on earth at the time he lived. Jesus had already performed a miracle. Nicodemus must have heard Jesus or about Him teaching in the temple and astounding the Jewish people of His knowledge of their Law as told in the Old Testament prophets and writings. Jesus didn't have formal seminary training or college. Nicodemus, fearing his companion teachers and rabbis, came to Him at night and said to Him that they knew He had come from God as a teacher for no one could do the signs that He was doing unless God was with Him.

Jesus answered and said to him, "Truly, truly, I say to you, unless one is born again, he cannot see the kingdom of God (John 3:3)." Note that this one response is the key to the spiritual rebirth.

Nicodemus said to Him, "How can a man be born when he is old? He cannot enter a second time into his mother's womb and be born, can he (John 3:4)?" Notice it says that Nicodemus was old physically and was thinking in human physical terms of being born again from his mother's body, which was what Jesus would now address.

Jesus answered, "Truly, truly, I say to you, unless one is born of water (physical birth) and the Spirit (spiritual birth) he cannot enter into the kingdom of God. That which is born of the flesh is flesh and that which is born of the Spirit is spirit." (John 3:5-6)

When Jesus spoke and said something twice, it meant to really pay attention. Note that Jesus said, "Truly, truly," twice in both of His responses to Nicodemus.

Jesus then went on to tell Nicodemus in (John 3:13-18), "No one has ascended into heaven, but He who descended from heaven: the Son of Man." Here He revealed where He came from.

He went on to give Nicodemus an illustration he could

understand from the Old Testament, which Nicodemus had studied. As Moses lifted up the serpent in the wilderness (Numbers 21:6-9), even so must the Son of Man be lifted up; so that whoever believes will in Him have eternal life. Then Jesus said the following, which many Christians often quote:

> "For God so loved the world, that He gave His only begotten Son, that whoever believes in Him shall not perish, but have eternal life (John 3:16)."

He goes on to say "For God did not send His Son into the world to judge the world, but that the world might be saved through Him. He who believes in Him is not judged; he who does not believe has been judged already because he has not believed in the name of the only begotten Son of God (John 3:17—18). It's interesting to me that God already knows what your and my responses will be because God is not bound by time; He knows the past, present, and future (Psalm 139:13-18), although it has to do with our free will in the current time when we are conscious and live and must make these decisions on our own accord.

Jesus goes on to give the reason some people respond to this spiritual rebirth and some don't.

"This is the judgement, that the Light has come into the world, and men loved the darkness rather than the Light, for their deeds were evil. For everyone who does evil hates the Light, and does not come to the Light for fear that his deeds will be exposed. But he who practices the truth comes to the Light, so that his deeds may be manifested as having been wrought in God (John 3:19-21)." This would then give Nicodemus an understanding of why some of his fellow associates would not respond to this eternal life-saving message.

So once we are born again, we have a supernatural perspective on why we are here and how we should live.

Ephesians 2:8-10 confirms that we are saved eternally and tells us why we are here: "For by grace you have been saved through faith; and that not of yourselves, it is the gift of God; not as a result of works (we can't earn it by our actions or deeds) so that no one may boast. For we are His workmanship, created in Christ Jesus for good works (why we are here), which God prepared beforehand so that we would walk in them."

This should encourage us to strive to do the works here on earth we were created to do, many of which are mentioned in the next chapter. We can only really have an understanding of these works after we are spiritually reborn. Basically, it's doing loving and kind things for others and looking to God for instruction and guidance.

Your ears will hear a word behind you, "This is the way, walk in it," whenever you turn to the right or to the left (Isaiah 30:21).

I will instruct you and teach you in the way which you should go; I will counsel you with My eye upon you (Psalm 32:8).

"Treat others the same way you want them to treat you." (Luke 6:31)

Lead others to God so that they can become spiritually reborn.

Chapter 8

OUTCOMES OF A SPIRITUAL REBIRTH

What should our responses be, and how should we live after a spiritual rebirth?

Second Corinthians 5:17-20 says we should show the love of God through our actions, bringing the knowledge of Him to others and encouraging them to know Him and come back to Him.

Ephesians 2:10 tells us we have been created for good works, so we should follow through with these works.

According to Romans 12:1-2, we should live in such a way that we are transformed in our thinking so that we may do the good and acceptable and perfect will of God.

In James 3:17, we should exhibit characteristics of wisdom

from above that are first pure, them peaceable, gentle, reasonable, full of mercy and good fruits, unwavering, without hypocrisy.

In Galatians 5:22-23, we find the outcome of our change is that we now exhibit love, joy, peace, patience, kindness, goodness, faithfulness, gentleness, and self-control.

According to Philippians 4:4-9, we should dwell on things that are true, honorable, right, pure, lovely, of good repute, excellence, and anything worthy of praise.

Second Peter 1:3-11 says since we have been given everything pertaining to life and godliness through a true knowledge of God, and God has given us precious and magnificent promises so that we may become partakers of the divine nature we should:

> Be diligent with our faith, have moral excellence, then knowledge, then self-control, then perseverance, then godliness, then brotherly kindness and then love. From our faith growing through multiple phases ultimately resulting in love and caring for others.

The apostle Peter said these things help assure we don't stumble, meaning entrance into the eternal kingdom of our Lord and Savior Jesus Christ will be abundantly supplied to us.

We are told in Romans 12:4-21 that we each have spiritual gifts of varying types as compared to a body and how the various parts work together. We should use these gifts to build up the spiritual body here on earth while we are alive.

In 2 Timothy 2:15 and 2 Timothy 3:16-17 we are encouraged

to study the Bible so that we can understand or handle it accurately and be adequately equipped for every good work.

Romans 15:1 we are told we who are strong ought to help those that are not.

Romans 15:7-14; 2:28-29; and 10:12 we learn that even though Christ came through the Jewish line, we are also accepted into God's plan of eternity as Gentiles.

Combined physical and spiritual timeline. (Note that the spiritual rebirth can occur almost anytime along the physical timeline, depending on when a person is prompted by God's Spirit and responds).

Stephen E. Lehnert, MD

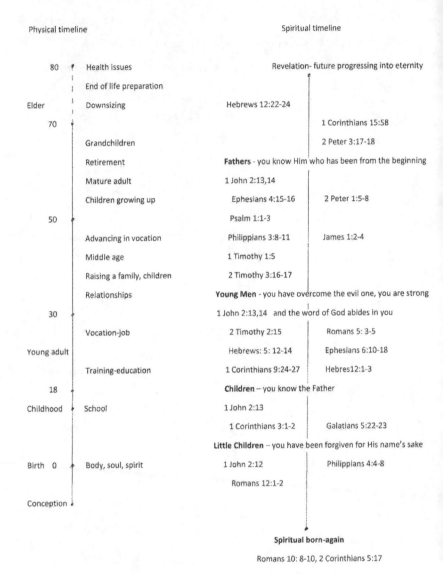

Physical timeline

Spiritual timeline

| 80 | Health issues | Revelation- future progressing into eternity |

End of life preparation

Elder — Downsizing — Hebrews 12:22-24

70

1 Corinthians 15:58

Grandchildren — 2 Peter 3:17-18

Retirement — **Fathers** - you know Him who has been from the beginning

Mature adult — 1 John 2:13,14

Children growing up — Ephesians 4:15-16 — 2 Peter 1:5-8

50 — Psalm 1:1-3

Advancing in vocation — Philippians 3:8-11 — James 1:2-4

Middle age — 1 Timothy 1:5

Raising a family, children — 2 Timothy 3:16-17

Relationships — **Young Men** - you have overcome the evil one, you are strong

30 — 1 John 2:13,14 and the word of God abides in you

Vocation-job — 2 Timothy 2:15 — Romans 5: 3-5

Young adult — Hebrews: 5: 12-14 — Ephesians 6:10-18

Training-education — 1 Corinthians 9:24-27 — Hebres12:1-3

18 — **Children** – you know the Father

Childhood — School — 1 John 2:13

1 Corinthians 3:1-2 — Galatians 5:22-23

Little Children -- you have been forgiven for His name's sake

Birth 0 — Body, soul, spirit — 1 John 2:12 — Philippians 4:4-8

Romans 12:1-2

Conception

Spiritual born-again

Romans 10: 8-10, 2 Corinthians 5:17

Chapter 9

WHAT IS THE CHURCH

What is a church, and what is its function?

Throughout history, many people have thought church is just a physical building where people meet, talk about Bible things, and get to know each other every Saturday or Sunday. Some people even go so far as to think that if they do these things faithfully, it will, "get them into heaven," and, "make them a good person." They feel like if they do it every so often, for example on special holidays like Easter or Christmas, they should be okay.

In actuality a church is a group of spiritually reborn people in Christ who meet together.

"I also say to you that you are Peter, and upon this rock I will build My church; and the gates of Hades will not overpower it (Matthew 16:18)."

A church has nothing to do with the physical building other

than it is a meeting site for the true church, which is actually composed of people.

Or do you not know that your body is a temple of the Holy Spirit who is in you, whom you have from God, and that you are not your own (1 Corinthians 6:19)?

For we are the temple of the living God; just as God said, "I will dwell in them and walk among them; and I will be their God, and they shall be My people (2 Corinthians 6:16)."

And for an entire year they met with the church and taught considerable numbers; and the disciples were first called Christians in Antioch (Acts 11:26).

Jesus Christ is the chief cornerstone of the building of people that make up the church.

Having been built on the foundation of the apostles and prophets, Christ Jesus Himself being the corner stone, in whom the whole building, being fitted together, is growing into a holy temple in the Lord, in whom you also are being built together into a dwelling of God in the Spirit (Ephesians 2:20-22).

Jesus said to them, "Did you never read the Scriptures, 'The stone which the builders rejected, this became the chief cornerstone; this came about from the Lord, and it is marvelous in our eyes (Matthew 21:42)'"?

The stone which the builders rejected has become the chief cornerstone. This is the Lord's doing; it is marvelous in our eyes (Psalm 118:22,23).

And coming to Him as to a living stone which has been rejected by men, but is choice and precious in the sight of God, you also as living stones, are being built up as a spiritual house for a holy priesthood, to offer up spiritual sacrifices acceptable to God through Jesus Christ. For this is contained in Scripture: "Behold, I lay in Zion a choice stone, a precious corner stone, and he who believes in Him will not be disappointed." This precious value, then, is for you who believe; but for those who disbelieve, "The stone which the builders rejected, this became the very cornerstone (1 Peter 2:4-7),"

We all fit together into the body of believers in Christ, which is considered to be the true church.

We are called together to encourage each other. (Hebrews 10:24-25).

Now you are Christ's body, and individually members of it (1 Corinthians 12:27).

Instructions are given on how we are to use our spiritual gifts. (1 Corinthians 12:1-27).

How are we to act in the church body? Speaking to one another in psalms and hymns and spiritual songs, singing and making melody with your heart to the Lord; always giving thanks for all things in the name of our Lord Jesus Christ to God, even the Father; and be subject to one another in the fear of Christ (Ephesians 5:19-21); Let the word of Christ richly dwell within you, with all wisdom teaching and admonishing one another with psalms and hymns and spiritual songs, singing with thankfulness in your hearts to God. Whatever you do in word or deed, do all in the name of the Lord Jesus, giving thanks through Him to God the Father (Colossians 3:16-17).

There are many churches that were not functioning properly as mentioned in the first part of Revelation, and the scripture gives instruction on the way seven churches (the people of these local churches in Asia) should conduct themselves as well as what they can look forward to in eternity (Revelation chapters 2 and 3). Consider the various church denominations today and how we might also struggle with some of these things as the churches in Asia at that time were struggling. Note that angels watch over churches, and the message in Revelation is to the angels watching over the churches.

If you look to become involved in a church after being born again, do the following. Look around you. Have you identified people in your travel through life that exhibit characteristics of a born-again person? Do they have a kindness and compassion for others that stands out? Are they quick to hear, slow to speak, and slow to anger? Do they exhibit love for others, joy, peace, patience, kindness, goodness, faithfulness, gentleness, and self-control? Are they the type of people who makes you take notice and find something special in the way they act toward others? Do they help people in need and come to the aid of others? When finding a person who can lead you to the right local church body, do they readily confess that Jesus Christ is Lord (test the spirits)? Are they actively involved in the church, using their God-given spiritual gifts to help and build up others?

If someone were to look at you, would they find these same characteristics?

Understand that there is no perfect, sinless human being other than Jesus Christ. But do others express at least some of these characteristics? Can they encourage you to do good deeds (Hebrews 10:24-25)? Are they part of a local church that you could belong to and grow with? Are they meeting the needs of others? Can they help meeting your and your family's needs?

Chapter 10

GLIMPSES OF THE SPIRITUAL
REALM IN THE PHYSICAL REALM

What is happening in the spiritual realm, and what is the spiritual realm as it relates to the physical realm?

Many of us will never have a clue of what is really happening around us in the spiritual realm unless the Spirit of God enlightens us for a specific reason or purpose. There are some verses in the Old Testament as well as the New Testament that give a glimpse of things in the angelic realm that is part of the spiritual realm. For instance, in the Old Testament, when there were wars against the Jewish people, God placed prophets amid His people to help and instruct them.

In 2 Kings 6:8-18 there is an account of a war with Arameans fighting Israel. The prophet Elisha would counsel the king of Israel about the plans of the Arameans. God would reveal the

Aramean king's whereabouts to the prophet Elisha supernaturally, and he would convey this information to the king of Israel so he could prepare himself. So an army was sent out to capture Elisha, and the Arameans' horses and chariots surrounded the city where Elisha was. Elisha's servant was scared and asked him, "What shall we do?" Elisha answered, "Do not fear, for those who are with us are more than those who are with them." Then Elisha prayed and said, "O Lord, I pray, open his eyes that he may see."

And the Lord opened the servant's eyes and he saw the mountains were full of horses and chariots of fire all around Elisha. When they came down to him, Elisha prayed to the Lord and said, "Strike this people with blindness, I pray." So He struck the army with blindness according to the word of Elisha.

The story goes on as to how Elisha then led the blinded enemy army to Samaria and prayed that their eyes would be reopened and they were right in front of the king of Israel. He goes on to say that the king of Israel fed them and then sent them on their way. They never warred with the king after that.

Most of us will not routinely see an angelic army of horses and chariots surrounding us, but understand this may actually be happening when God sees fit to protect us, His born-again believers.

"No weapon that is formed against you will prosper; and every tongue that accuses you in judgement you will condemn. This is the heritage of the servants of the Lord, and their vindication is from Me," declares the Lord (Isaiah 54:17).

There are destroying angels in the spiritual realm as David talks about in 1 Chronicles 21:16, when a plague was sent against

Israel for David taking a census with which God was displeased. David actually saw the angel of the Lord standing between earth and heaven, with his sword drawn in his hand stretched out over Jerusalem. Note David's response. Being terrified, David and the elders with him covered themselves in sackcloth and fell on their faces. In 1 Chronicles 21: 28—30 it notes that when the Lord had answered David, he offered a sacrifice there. David could not go to the appointed alter to offer a sacrifice in Gibeon and inquire of God because he was terrified by the sword of the angel of the Lord.

It is hard to comprehend these things without personal experience, but they exist. We may also be unaware of these things happening around us. Hebrews 13:1-2 tells us to love each other and do not neglect to show hospitality to strangers because we may have unknowingly entertained angels. Can you even imagine entertaining a supernatural angelic being in front of you in human form?

Heavenly spiritual events have occurred to people on earth. In Matthew 17:1-7, Jesus took Peter, James, and John up a high mountain and was transfigured before them, with Moses and Elijah appearing to them.

When the apostles were put in a public jail, an angel of the Lord opened the gates of the jail and told them to go stand and speak to the people in the temple about the whole message of this life. (Acts 5:18-20)

Several other examples have been recorded in the scriptures that one tends to gloss over without much thought and not give attention to and potentially are deceived by the evil one as not true. Can you actually picture three men being thrown into a fiery furnace and surviving with an angel of God in their midst protecting them? Note that the guards that threw the men in the furnace died from the intense heat.

Shadrach, Meshach and Abed-nego replied to the king. "O Nebuchadnezzar, we do not need to give you and answer concerning this matter. If it be so, our God whom we serve is able to deliver us from the furnace of blazing fire; and He will deliver us out of your hand, O king. But even if He does not, let it be known to you, O king, that we are not going to serve your gods or worship the golden image that you have set up." Then Nebuchadnezzar was filled with wrath, and his facial expression was altered toward Shadrach, Meshach and Abed-nego. He answered by giving orders to heat the furnace seven times more than it was usually heated. He commanded certain valiant warriors who were in his army to tie up Shadrach, Meshach and Abed-nego in order to cast them into the furnace of blazing fire. Then these men were tied up in their trousers, their coats, their caps and their other clothes, and were cast into the midst of the furnace of blazing fire. For this reason, because the king's command was urgent and the furnace had been made extremely hot, the flame of the fire slew those men who carried up Shadrach, Meshach and Abed-nego. But these three men, Shadrach, Meshach and Abed-nego, fell into the midst of the furnace of blazing fire still tied up. Then Nebuchadnezzar the king was astounded and stood up in haste; he said to his high officials, "Was it not three men we cast bound into the midst of the fire?" They replied to the king, "Certainly, O king." He said, "Look! I see four men loosed and walking about in the midst of the fire without harm, and the appearance of the fourth is like a son of the gods!" Then Nebuchadnezzar came near to the door of the furnace of blazing fire; he responded and said, "Shadrach, Meshach and Abed-nego, come out, you servants of the Most High God, and come here!" Then Shadrach, Meshach and Abed-nego came out of the midst of the fire. The satraps, the prefects, the governors and the king's high officials gathered around and saw in regard to these men that the fire had no effect on the bodies of these men nor was the hair of their head singed, nor were there trousers damaged, nor had the smell of fire even come upon them. Nebuchadnezzar responded and said, "Blessed be the God of Shadrach, Meshach and Abed-nego, who has sent His angel and delivered His servants who put their trust in Him, violating the king's command, and yielded up their bodies so as not to serve or worship any god except their own God. Therefore I make a decree that any people, nation or tongue that speaks anything offensive against the God of Shadrach, Meshach and Abednego shall be torn limb from limb and their houses reduced to a rubbish heap, inasmuch as there is no other god who is able to deliver in this way." Then the king caused Shadrach, Meshach and Abed-nego to prosper in the province of Babylon (Daniel 3: 16-30).

Consider what would happen if you were thrown into a den of ravenous lions all night as Daniel was without undergoing harm? Note also that his accusers ended up being eaten alive when the king threw them in the den after Daniel was recovered.

Then the commissioners and satraps came by agreement to the king and spoke to him as follows: "King Darius, live forever! All the commissioners of the kingdom, the prefects and the satraps, the high officials and the governors have consulted together that the king should establish a statute and enforce an injunction that anyone who makes a petition to any god or man besides you, O king, for thirty days, shall be cast into the lions' den. Now, O king, establish the injunction and sign the document so that it may not be changed, according to the law of the Medes and Persians, which may not be revoked." Therefore king Darius signed the document, that is the injunction. Now when Daniel knew that the document was signed, he entered his house (now in his roof chamber he had windows open toward Jerusalem); and he continued kneeling on his knees three times a day, praying and giving thanks before his God, as he had been doing previously. Then these men came by agreement and found Daniel making petition and supplication before his God. Then they approached and spoke before the king about the king's injunction, "Did you not sign an injunction that any man who makes a petition to any god or man besides you, O king, for thirty days is to be cast into the lions' den?" The king replied, "The statement is true, according to the law of the Medes and Persians, which may not be revoked." Then they answered and spoke before the king, "Daniel, who is one of the exiles from Judah, pays no attention to you, O king, or to the injunction which you signed, but keeps making his petition three times a day." Then as soon as the king heard this statement, he was deeply distressed and set his mind on delivering Daniel; and even until sunset he kept exerting himself to rescue him. Then these men came by agreement to the king and said to the king, "Recognize, O king, that it is a law of the Medes and the Persians that no injunction or statue which the king establishes may be changed." Then the king gave orders, and Daniel was brought in and cast into the lions' den. The king spoke and said to Daniel, "Your God whom you constantly serve will Himself deliver you." A stone was brought and laid over the mouth of the den; and the king sealed it with his own signet ring and with the signet rings of his nobles, so that nothing would be changed in regard to Daniel. Then the king went off to his palace and spent the night fasting, and no entertainment was brought before him; and his sleep fled from him. Then the king arose at dawn, at the break of day, and went in haste to the lions' den. When he had come near the den to Daniel, he cried out with a troubled voice. The king spoke and said to Daniel, "Daniel servant of the living God, has your God, whom you constantly serve, been able to deliver you from the lions?" Then Daniel spoke to the king, "O king, live forever! My God sent His angel and shut the lions' mouths and they have not harmed me, inasmuch as I was found innocent before Him, and also toward you, O king, I have committed no crime." Then the king was very pleased and gave orders for Daniel to be taken up out of the den. So Daniel was taken up out of the den and no injury whatever was found on him, because he had trusted in his God. The king then gave orders, and they brought those men who had maliciously accused Daniel and they cast them, their children and their wives into the lions' den; and they had not reached the bottom of the den before the lions overpowered them and crushed all their bones. Then Darius the king wrote to all the peoples, nations and men of every language who were living in all the land: "May your peace abound! I make a decree that in all the dominion of my kingdom men are to fear and tremble before the God of Daniel; For He is the living God and enduring forever, and His kingdom is one which will not be destroyed, and His dominion will be forever. "He delivers and rescues and performs signs and wonders in heaven and on earth, Who has also delivered Daniel from the power of the lions." So this Daniel enjoyed success in the reign of Darius and in the reign of Cyrus the Persian (Daniel 6: 6-28).

Chapter 11

WAR IN THE SPIRITUAL REALM

What are spiritual battles, and who and what are involved?

Paul, a servant of God proclaiming the good news of Christ and being born again, had some exceptional revelations as he notes in 2 Corinthians 12:1-7 that boasting is necessary, though it is not profitable; but I will go on to visions and revelations of the Lord. I know a man in Christ who fourteen years ago—whether in the body I do not know, God knows—such a man was caught up to the third heaven. And I know how such a man—whether in the body or apart from the body I do not know, God knows—was caught up into Paradise and heard inexpressible words, which a man is not permitted to speak. On behalf of such a man I will boast; but on my own behalf I will not boast, except in regard to my weaknesses. For if I do wish to boast I will not be foolish, for I will be speaking the truth; but I refrain from this, so that no one will credit me with more than he sees in me or hears from me.

He mentions due to the exceptional revelations he was given a thorn in his flesh so he would not exalt himself.

Because of the surpassing greatness of the revelations for this reason, to keep me from exalting myself, there was given me a thorn in the flesh, a messenger of Satan to torment me—to keep me from exalting myself! Concerning this I implored the Lord three times that it might leave me. And He said to me, "My grace is sufficient for you, for power is perfected in weakness." Most gladly, therefore, I will rather boast about my weaknesses, so that the power of Christ may dwell in me. Therefore I am well content with weaknesses, with insults, with distresses, with persecutions, with difficulties, for Christ's sake; for when I am weak, then I am strong (2 Corinthians 12:7-10).

This same man describes to us what is involved in spiritual warfare as someone who was fighting in this battle. In Ephesians 6, Paul is telling the church in Ephesus that we should be strong in the Lord and in the strength of His might. This is done by putting on the full armor of God so that we will be able to stand against the schemes of the devil. What is the full armor of God?

Our struggle is not against flesh and blood (physical) but against rulers, powers, world forces of this darkness, and against the spiritual forces of wickedness in the heavenly places (spiritual).

According to Ephesians 6:10-17, the armor we can put on to protect us in the spiritual realm consists of:

1. Gird our loins with truth
2. The breastplate of righteousness
3. Cover our feet with the preparation of the gospel of peace

4. The shield of faith
5. The helmet of salvation
6. The sword of the Spirit, which is the Word of God

The six things above give us defensive and offensive spiritual weaponry.

Our battles are not against flesh and blood but spiritual warfare.

> For though we walk in the flesh, we do not war according to the flesh, for the weapons of our warfare are not of the flesh but divinely powerful for the destruction of fortresses. We are destroying speculations and every lofty thing raised up against the knowledge of God, and we are taking every thought captive to the obedience of Christ, and we are ready to punish all disobedience, whenever your obedience is complete (2 Corinthians 10:3-6).

These include thoughts that come into our minds against the knowledge of God that the evil one tries to distract us with and derail our spiritual growth. This might be likened to a tumor or cancer in our physical bodies or failing organ systems that threaten our growth or life. Our thoughts ultimately determine our responses or actions.

In fact, Paul told the Corinthians that he was with them in weakness and in fear and in much trembling (physical). His message and his preaching were not in persuasive words of wisdom but in the demonstration of the Spirit and of power (spiritual) so that their faith would not rest on the wisdom of men but on the power of God.

First Corinthians 2:9-11 tells us, "Things which eye has not seen and ear has not heard (in the physical), and which have not entered the heart of man, all that God has prepared (spiritual) for those who love Him." For to us God has revealed them through the Spirit; for the Spirit searches all things, even the depths of God (spiritual). For who among men knows the thoughts of a man except the spirit of the man which is in him? Even so the thoughts of God no one knows except the Spirit of God.

The Bible goes on to say that: Now we have received, not the spirit of the world, but the Spirit who is from God (being born again), so that we may know the things freely given to us by God, which things we also speak, not in words taught by human wisdom, but in those taught by the Spirit, combining spiritual thoughts with spiritual words (1 Corinthians 2:12-13).

Note also that: A natural man does not accept the things of the Spirit of God, for they are foolishness to him; and he cannot understand them, because they are spiritually appraised. But he who is spiritual (born again) appraises all things, yet he himself is appraised by no one. For who has known the mind of the Lord that he will instruct Him? But we have the mind of Christ (1 Corinthians 2:14-16).

There is great encouragement in the book of John where it tells us about God's character, what He is like and what He asks us to do.

"A new commandment I give to you, that you love one

another, even as I have loved you, that you also love one another. By this all men will know that you are My disciples, if you have love for one another." (John 13:34-35)

He also tells us what we can expect as His born-again believers and how He is with us in the book of John, especially chapters 14 through 16. His prayer for us as disciples in the world and for our future glory in the heavenly realm is shared in chapter 17.

These are important chapters in the book of John to read, think about and incorporate into your daily thinking and life.

Chapter 12

WHEN BAD THINGS HAPPEN

What happens when something goes wrong?

How do people deal with poor health, loss, tragedy, addictions, broken relationships, and other bad things that come their way? There may be many reasons for things happening around us that sometimes involve us personally. Some of these are to test us.

Consider it all joy, my brethren, when you encounter various trials, knowing that the testing of your faith produces endurance. And let endurance have its perfect result, so that you may be perfect and complete, lacking in nothing (James 1:2-4).

Some of these events are hard to understand and deal with. As a spiritually reborn person, we have the assurance of God's ultimate intercession for us and that we will ultimately conquer through Him who loves us.

What then shall we say to these things? If God is for us, who is against us? He who did not spare His own Son, but delivered

Him over for us all, how will He not also with Him freely give us all things? Who will bring a charge against God's elect? God is the one who justifies; who is the one who condemns? Christ Jesus is He who died, yes, rather who was raised, who is at the right hand of God, who also intercedes for us. Who will separate us from the love of Christ? Will tribulation, or distress, or persecution, or famine, or nakedness, or peril, or sword? Just as it is written, "For Your sake we are being put to death all day long; we are considered as sheep to be slaughtered." But in all these things we overwhelmingly conquer through Him who loved us. For I am convinced that neither death, nor life, nor angels, nor principalities, nor things present, nor things to come, nor powers, nor height, nor depth, nor any other created thing, will be able to separate us from the love of God, which is in Christ Jesus our Lord (Romans 8:31-39). Nothing can separate us from His love.

Bad things come from our inherent human natures and sins. Every good thing comes from God.

Every good thing given and every perfect gift is from above, coming down from the Father of lights, with whom there is no variation or shifting shadow (James 1:17).

Sometimes terrible things happen to people with no apparent reason, at least in terms that our human minds can comprehend. After noting that God causes all things to work together for good to those who love God, to those who are called according to His purpose (Romans 8:28), consider some events that took place in the Bible that were seemingly hard to understand for people at the time.

In Luke 13:4, Christ asked the people if they supposed that

the eighteen people on whom the tower of Siloam fell and were killed were worse sinners than all the men who lived in Jerusalem. He said, "I tell you, no, but unless you repent, you will all likewise perish."

A modern-day translation might be, "Do you think that all the people (2,753) who died in the Twin Towers were singled out to die because of who they were or what they did? The response to us might be, "No, but unless our nation repents of its evil deeds, we will all likewise perish."

In John 9:1-5, there was a man born blind. Christ's disciples asked Him, "Rabbi, who sinned, this man or his parents, that he would be born blind?" Jesus's response was, "It was neither that this man sinned, nor his parents; but it was so that the works of God might be displayed in him. We must work the works of Him who sent Me as long as it is day; night is coming when no man can work. While I am in the world, I am the light of the world."

Another example is Psalm 106:6-7, 13-14, 19, 21-29 which says, We have sinned like our fathers, we have committed iniquity, we have behaved wickedly. Our fathers in Egypt did not understand Your wonders; They did not remember Your abundant kindnesses, but rebelled by the sea, at the Red Sea. They quickly forgot His works; They did not wait for His counsel, but craved intensely in the wilderness, and tempted God in the desert. They made a calf in Horeb and worshipped a molten image. They forgot God their Savior, Who had done great things in Egypt, wonders in the land of Ham and awesome things by the Red Sea. Therefore He said He would destroy them, had not Moses His chosen one stood in the breach before Him, to turn away His wrath from destroying them. Then they despised the pleasant land; they did not believe His word, but grumbled in their tents; they did not listen to the voice of the Lord. Therefore He swore to them that He would cast them down in the wilderness, and that He would cast their seed among the nations and scatter them in the lands. They joined themselves also to Baal-peor, and ate sacrifices offered to the dead. Thus they provoked Him to anger with their deeds, and the plague broke out among them.

A plague was sent among the Israelites who had sinned and forgotten the abundant kindness of God to them, as well as forgetting His works and not waiting for His counsel, craving, becoming envious, worshipping an image and not God, and finally forgetting God.

Could the modern-day coronavirus-19 pandemic affecting our nation and the world be in part related to our nation, which was originally founded on God and His scriptural principles ("One nation, under God, with liberty and justice for all") turning away from God.

Consider that He may be giving our nation a wake-up call to repent and turn back to Him in the way our nation acts toward others and each other. To make our nation great again should be based on the principles given in Matthew 23:11-12: "But the greatest among you shall be your servant." And the warning, "Whoever exalts himself shall be humbled." Consider how our nation has come to the aid of so many people around the world in the past, standing up for what is right when the people of our country were following biblical principles and God causing our nation to prosper. The world leadership and admiration that our country has had in the past seems to be fading as our nation turns away from scriptural principles. Additional references to who is greatest are the following.

At that time the disciples came to Jesus and said, "Who then is greatest in the kingdom of heaven?" And He called a child to Himself and set him before them, and said, "Truly I say to you, unless you are converted and become like children, you will not enter the kingdom of heaven. Whoever then humbles himself as this child, he is the greatest in the kingdom of heaven. And whoever receives one such child in My name receives Me (Matthew 18:1-5);"

And there arose also a dispute among them as to which one of them was regarded to be the greatest. And He said to them, "The kings of the Gentiles lord it over them; and those who have authority over them are called 'Benefactors.' But it is not this way with you, but the one who is the greatest among you must become like the youngest, and the leader like the servant. For who is greater, the one who reclines at the table or the one who serves? Is it not the one who reclines at the table? But I am among you as the one who serves (Luke 22:24-27).

Chapter 13

OUR ETERNAL INHERITANCE

What are we worth?

I'm not talking about your net worth of physical money and physical possessions, your credit score, or your physical body, which are the measures many people use to evaluate us these days. By the way, these won't mean a lot to us when we are close to physical death. After all, "You can't take it with you."

Let's look into the eternal realm and see what we will have as an inheritance having been born again into spiritual life as noted in the Bible. Please consider the following references and think about them often. Writing these things down and thinking about them should give you continued encouragement as you grow spiritually and prepare you for life eternal.

In Him also we have obtained an inheritance, having been predestined according to His purpose who works all things after the counsel of His will, to the end that we who were the first to hope in Christ would be to the praise of His glory. In Him, you also, after listening to the message of truth, the gospel of your salvation—having also believed, you were sealed in Him with the Holy Spirit of promise, who is given as a pledge of our inheritance, with a view to the redemption of God's own possession, to the praise of His glory (Ephesians 1:11-14).

For this reason also, since the day we heard of it, we have not ceased to pray for you and to ask that you may be filled with the knowledge of His will in all spiritual wisdom and understanding, so that you will walk in a manner worthy of the Lord, to please Him in all respects, bearing fruit in every good work and increasing in the knowledge of God; strengthened with all power, according to His glorious might, for the attaining of all steadfastness and patience; joyously giving thanks to the Father, who has qualified us to share in the inheritance of the saints in Light (Colossians 1 :9-12).

Whatever you do, do your work heartily, as for the Lord rather than for men, knowing that from the Lord you will receive the reward of the inheritance. It is the Lord Christ whom you serve (Colossians 3:23,24).

For this reason He is the mediator of a new covenant, so that, since a death has taken place for the redemption of the transgressions that were committed under the first covenant, those who have been called may receive the promise of the eternal inheritance (Hebrews 9:15).

Blessed be the God and Father of our Lord Jesus Christ, who according to His great mercy has caused us to be born again to a living hope through the resurrection of Jesus Christ from the dead, to obtain an inheritance which is imperishable and undefiled and will not fade away, reserved in heaven for you, who are protected by the power of God through faith for a salvation ready to be revealed in the last time (1 Peter 1:3-5).

Blessed be the God and Father of our Lord Jesus Christ, who has blessed us with every spiritual blessing in the heavenly places in Christ, just as He chose us in Him before the foundation of the world, that we would be holy and blameless before Him. In love He predestined us to adoption as sons through Jesus Christ to Himself, according to the kind intention of His will, to the praise of the glory of His grace, which He freely bestowed on us in the Beloved. In Him we have redemption through His blood, the forgiveness of our trespasses, according to the riches of His grace which He lavished on us. In all wisdom and insight He made known to us the mystery of His will, according to His kind intention which He purposed in Him with a view to an administration suitable to the fullness of the times, that is, the summing up of all things in Christ, things in the heavens and things on the earth (Ephesians 1: 3-10).

Physical timeline | Spiritual timeline

Physical timeline		Spiritual timeline
80	Health issues	Revelation- future progressing into eternity
	End of life preparation	
Elder	Downsizing	Hebrews 12:22-24
70		1 Corinthians 15:58
	Grandchildren	2 Peter 3:17-18
	Retirement	**Fathers** - you know Him who has been from the beginning
	Mature adult	1 John 2:13,14
	Children growing up	Ephesians 4:15-16 2 Peter 1:5-8
50		Psalm 1:1-3
	Advancing in vocation	Philippians 3:8-11 James 1:2-4
	Middle age	1 Timothy 1:5
	Raising a family, children	2 Timothy 3:16-17
	Relationships	**Young Men** - you have overcome the evil one, you are strong
30		1 John 2:13,14 and the word of God abides in you
	Vocation-job	2 Timothy 2:15 Romans 5: 3-5
Young adult		Hebrews: 5: 12-14 Ephesians 6:10-18
	Training-education	1 Corinthians 9:24-27 Hebres12:1-3
18		**Children** – you know the Father
Childhood	School	1 John 2:13
		1 Corinthians 3:1-2 Galatians 5:22-23
		Little Children – you have been forgiven for His name's sake
Birth 0	Body, soul, spirit	1 John 2:12 Philippians 4:4-8
		Romans 12:1-2
Conception		

Spiritual born-again

Romans 10: 8-10, 2 Corinthians 5:17

Chapter 14

LOOKING AHEAD

What do we have to look forward to?

Psalm 16:11 says,

> You will make known to me the path of life;
> In Your presence is fullness of joy;
> In Your right hand there are pleasures forever.

Knowing the right path to take in life and experiencing the fullness of joy and pleasures forever. Can you think of anything better? In eternity we will have new bodies, although we will still be recognized as who we are (1 Corinthians 15:42-49, 50-58).

How then should we live?

A spiritual timeline should show our growth, just like a physical timeline (see preceding page). Growing spiritually begins with basic things, like reading the Bible (God's Word as revealed by the prophets and men inspired by God), meditating on the Word, and incorporating it into our lives (memorizing specific verses). As we do this, we find practical applications for what we are learning and put things to work. At the same time, we are able to communicate with God through prayer, and the Holy Spirit intercedes for us, even if we don't know exactly what to say when praying.

In the same way the Spirit also helps our weakness; for we do not know how to pray as we should, but the Spirit Himself intercedes for us with groanings too deep for words; and He who searches the hearts knows what the mind of the Spirit is, because He intercedes for the saints according to the will of God (Romans 8:26-27).

So God actually hears and receives the messages of our hearts when we pray to Him.

Getting involved in a local church is the next step to growing, learning, encouraging, and being encouraged by others. This is referred to as the body of Christ—not an actual literal building, but spiritually reborn Christians. The literal brick and mortar church building is where the actual church (people) many times meet. They can also meet in homes or other places. Relationships develop, and continued growth occurs with the type of people who can be really true friends looking out for each other with the right motivations.

By meeting together, we can also encourage each other with psalms, hymns, and spiritual songs. We can really start to understand what the spiritual world is all about.

Therefore be careful how you walk, not as unwise men but as wise, making the most of your time, because the days are evil. So then do not be foolish, but understand what the will of the Lord is. And do not get drunk with wine, for this is dissipation, but be filled with the Spirit, speaking to one another in psalms and hymns and spiritual songs, singing and making melody with your heart to the Lord; always giving thanks for all things in the name of our Lord Jesus Christ to God, even the Father; and be subject to one another in the fear of Christ (Ephesians 5:15-21).

Let the word of Christ richly dwell within you, with all wisdom teaching and admonishing one another with psalms and hymns and spiritual songs, singing with thankfulness in your hearts to God (Colossians 3:16).

God's people care for each other with acts of kindness and helping people in need with the right motivation, not seeking personal gain, and spiritual growth takes place. In the end, these born-again people are gaining a whole lot more. Acts 20:35 notes it is more blessed to give than to receive. Meeting together in buildings with musical instruments and worship teams can be a time of songs and celebration to the God who created us and a time of giving thanks to God for what He has done.

When prompted by the Spirit, people are baptized as a public profession of their faith. This is a symbolic representation of leaving their old non-born-again life and coming up out of the water that represents new life.

In the Old Testament, Moses wrote about the importance of teaching our children.

"Hear, O Israel! The Lord is our God, the Lord is One! You

shall love the Lord your God with all your heart and with all your soul and with all your might. These words which I am commanding you today, shall be on your heart. You shall teach them diligently to your sons and shall talk of them when you sit in your house and when you walk by the way and when you lie down and when you rise up. You shall bind them as a sign on your hand and they shall be as frontals on your forehead. You shall write them on the doorposts of your house and on your gates (Deuteronomy 6:4-9).

"You shall therefore impress these words of mine on your heart and on your soul; and you shall bind them as a sign on your hand, and they shall be as frontals on your forehead. You shall teach them to your sons, talking of them when you sit in your house and when you walk along the road and when you lie down and when you rise up. You shall write them on the doorposts of your house and on your gates, so that your days and the days of your sons may be multiplied on the land which the Lord swore to your fathers to give them, as long as the heavens remain above the earth. For if you are careful to keep all this commandment which I am commanding you to do, to love the Lord your God, to walk in all His ways and hold fast to Him, then the Lord will drive out all these nations from before you, and you will dispossess nations greater and mightier than you (Deuteronomy 11:18-23).

And the results of doing so to pass this spiritual message to our future generations.

"Then it shall come about when the Lord your God brings you into the land which He swore to your fathers, Abraham, Isaac and Jacob, to give you, great and splendid cities which you did not build, and houses full of all good things which you did not fill, and hewn cisterns which you did not dig, vineyards and olive trees which you did not plant, and you eat and are satisfied, then watch yourself, that you do not forget the Lord who brought you from the land of Egypt, out of the house of slavery. You shall fear only the Lord your God; and you shall worship Him and swear by His name. You shall not follow other gods, any of the gods of the peoples who surround you (Deuteronomy 6:10-14).

Finally determining and developing the spiritual gifts God has given us in the spiritual realm will help us in building the spiritual body of Christ and accomplish things of eternal value.

Now concerning spiritual gifts, brethren, I do not want you to be unaware. You know that when you were pagans, you were led astray to the mute idols, however you were led. Therefore I make known to you that no one speaking by the Spirit of God says, "Jesus is accursed"; and no one can say, "Jesus is Lord," except by the Holy Spirit. Now there are varieties of gifts, but the same Spirit. And there are varieties of ministries, and the same Lord. There are varieties of effects, but the same God who works all things in all persons. But to each one is given the manifestations of the Spirit for the common good. For to one is given the word of wisdom through the Spirit and to another the word of knowledge according to the same Spirit; to another faith by the same Spirit, and to another gifts of healing by the one Spirit, and to another the effecting of miracles, and to another prophecy, and to another the distinguishing of spirits, to another various kinds of tongues, and to another the interpretations of tongues. But one and the same Spirit works all these things, distributing to each one individually as He wills. For even as the body is one and yet has many members, and all the members of the body, though they are many, are one body, so also is Christ. For by one Spirit we were all baptized into one body, whether Jews or Greeks, whether slaves or free, and we were all made to drink of one Spirit. For the body is not one member but many (1 Corinthians 12:1-14). (see also 1 Corinthians 12:15-26).

This will help us live and enjoy life to the fullest possible here and now, giving purpose and meaning to our lives and the eternal rewards we have to look forward to.

All this being said, consider it a preparation for eternity in the presence of God and being able to function with the tasks He has planned for us in the eternal realm with our new heavenly bodies and responsibilities.

But someone will say," How are the dead raised? And with what kind of body do they come?" You fool! That which you sow does not come to life unless it dies; and that which you sow, you do not sow the body which is to be, but a bare grain, perhaps of wheat or of something else. But God gives it a body just as He wished, and to each of the seeds a body of its own. All flesh is not the same flesh, but there is one flesh of men, and another flesh of beasts, and another flesh of birds, and another of fish. There are also heavenly bodies and earthly bodies, but the glory of the heavenly is one, and the glory of the earthly is another. There is one glory of the sun, and another glory of the moon, and another glory of the stars; for star differs from star in glory. So also is the resurrection of the dead. It is sown a perishable body, it is raised an imperishable body; it is sown in dishonor, it is raised in glory;

it is sown in weakness, it is raised in power; it is sown a natural body, it is raised a spiritual body. If there is a natural body, there is also a spiritual body. So also it is written, "The first man, Adam, became a living soul." The last Adam became a life-giving spirit. However, the spiritual is not first, but the natural; then the spiritual. The first man is from the earth, earthy; the second man is from heaven. As is the earthy, so also are those who are earthy; and as is the heavenly, so also those who are heavenly. Just as we have borne the image of the earthy, we will also bear the image of the heavenly (1 Corinthians 15:35-49).

Many of those who sleep in the dust of the ground will awake, those to everlasting life, but the others to disgrace and everlasting contempt. Those who have insight will shine brightly like the brightness of the expanse of heaven, and those who lead the many to righteousness, like the stars forever and ever (Daniel 12:2-3).

Epilogue

WORDS OF ENCOURAGEMENT

Many of us may be thinking, *I am older and advanced in years. I don't think I could ever attain the person I was meant to be.*

Please consider the parable of the laborers in the vineyard found in Matthew 20:1-16.

"For the kingdom of heaven is like a landowner who went out early in the morning to hire laborers for his vineyard. When he had agreed with the laborers for a denarius for the day, he sent them into his vineyard. And he went out about the third hour and saw others standing idle in the market place; and to those he said, 'You also go into the vineyard, and whatever is right I will give you.' And so they went. Again he went out about the sixth and the ninth hour, and did the same thing. And about the eleventh hour he went out and found others standing around; and he said to them, 'Why have you been standing here idle all day long?' They said to him, 'Because no one hired us.' He said to them, 'You go into the vineyard too.' "When evening came, the owner of the vineyard said to his foreman, 'Call the laborers and pay them their wages, beginning with the last group to the first.' When those hired about the eleventh hour came, each one received a denarius. When those hired first came, they thought that they would receive more; but each of them also received a denarius. When they received it, they grumbled at the landowner, saying, 'These last men have worked only one hour, and you have made them equal to us who have borne the burden and the scorching heat of the day.' But he answered and said to one of them, 'Friend, I am doing you no wrong; did you not agree with me for a denarius? Take what is yours and go, but I wish to give to this last man the same as to you. Is it not lawful for me to do what I wish with my own? Or is your eye envious because I am generous?' So the last shall be first, and the first last."

I mention this parable to note that one should not be discouraged if he or she becomes spiritually reborn at a later stage in life and then called to the work of God in the little time the person may have left in this physical life. This parable should be an encouragement to you to work the best you can with the time you have left on earth to do the work of God as He has called us. After all, God has blessed us with every spiritual blessing in the heavenly places in Christ (Ephesians 1:3).

Please take a moment to read Ephesians 1:1-23 and Colossians 1:1-23. Meditate and reflect on these verses and incorporate them into the reality of who you are once you have been born again spiritually, whether at the first hour or the eleventh hour. These are also excellent verses to memorize and use against the spiritual warfare of the evil one when he puts thoughts in your mind that you are not good enough or worthy to be with God in His presence. Consider and marvel at these precious and magnificent promises as recorded in the scriptures.

I really encourage you to use this short book as a survival guide and as a springboard to launch out and discover the Bible and become involved in the body of Christ here on earth after you are born again so that in eternity in the heavenly realm, you can look back and see that your labor was not in vain, and you will enjoy the precious and magnificent promises we have as born-again believers in Jesus Christ. Periodically check your growth along the spiritual growth chart, and look at the good works you are producing to help others. Remember to reflect on what you're worth.

Journal

Key Points of Growth in the Spiritual Life

'Not by might nor by power, but by My Spirit,' says the Lord of hosts (Zechariah 4:6).

My spiritual rebirth: _____

Spiritual growth plan: Read: _____

Reflect and think about: _____

Memorize: _____

Pray and communicate: _____

Apply to life: _____

Baptism: _____

Church body: _____

My spiritual gifts: _____

Special spiritual insights God has revealed to me: _____

_____

My spiritual relationships with others: _____

Those I have helped become spiritually reborn: _____

My Survival Tool Kit and Weapons

Memorized verses: _____

My Prayer List

Persons, requests, answers: _____

Wisdom from Above (James 3:17): _____

_____

Printed in the United States
By Bookmasters